The Nehemiah Challenge

Rebuilding the Broken Gates of Your Life

Dr. Craig D. Hayes

Sermon To Book
www.sermontobook.com

The Nehemiah Challenge / Dr. Craig D. Hayes
ISBN-13: 978-1-945793-63-9
ISBN-10: 1-945793-63-5

First, I dedicate this book to my Lord and Savior, Jesus Christ—all glory belongs to You!

To my loving wife, Shannon, and children—Endia, Sommer, Craig II, Lauren, Madyson, Eryn—you have supported me every step of the way.

To my loving mother, Pollie, and late father, Jerrett Hayes—I pray I continue to make you proud.

And to the greatest church family, CrossingPoint Christian Church—you have uplifted me in prayer and made pastoring a pleasure.

May God continue to bless you as much as you have blessed me.

Carpe diem en Christo,

Craig D. Hayes

CONTENTS

The Task at Hand 3

Rebuild Your Gates 7

A Firm Foundation 21

Courage in the Lord 37

Hold Your Ground Against the Enemy 51

The Truth Will Set You Free 63

Forgotten Testimony 77

It's Now or Never 89

Rise to the Challenge 103

Molded by God 117

Live in Freedom 129

Notes 131

About the Author 132

The Task at Hand

*So we built the wall. And all the wall was joined together
to half its height, for the people had a mind to work.*
—Nehemiah 4:6

What does it take to rebuild a life that has been invaded and conquered by the enemy? What does it take to reconstruct boundaries that have been destroyed? What does it take to reestablish a life focused on the truth of Christ? What does it take to be a shining example of love, perseverance, and vigilance while under threat of attack?

Like Nehemiah, we have a rebuilding project ahead of us if we are seeking to be disciples of Christ. We will need courage and a firm foundation in God's Word, and we will need a clear understanding of God's truth and how it differs from the messages being fed to us by the world. As we rebuild the walls of our lives, we will learn to trust God and His Word. As we are challenged to share His truth with younger generations, faith in Christ will become the lasting legacy we pass along.

Nehemiah undertook his own rebuilding process thousands of years ago, but his calling and his challenges resonate with us today (Nehemiah 2:1–5). And throughout Scripture, we find stories and exhortations that outline the path to abundant life and meaningful purpose in our walk with Christ.

The Bible shows us the way to true freedom and communion with God. Throughout this book, we will explore the biblical truths that will enable us to walk in the freedom Christ purchased for us. At the end of each chapter, workbook sections will help you unpack these truths and apply them to your life. (Feel free to write in the workbook section or in a separate journal or notebook.)

The use of the metaphor of walls in this book may strike you as unusual at first—after all, Christians tend to think of building walls as something negative. We are used to being told from the pulpit and in Christian media that we should not build walls but bridges. Putting up walls is problematic because it keeps us from relating to others and does not allow us to make genuine connections. If we put up walls in this sense, we choose to isolate ourselves from other believers and open our lives to attack from Satan.

However, in this book, based on the biblical account of Nehemiah, we discuss a different kind of wall: spiritual walls that protect and defend our faith, which are of the utmost importance. As believers, we need to build walls that strengthen our spiritual position in Christ and help us stand against Satan.

In this sense, walls around our hearts are necessary to protect us from the enemy, in the same manner that the walls of an ancient city protected its people from outside attack. Our defenses need to be strong so we can guard our hearts and lives for God, defending our faith and standing strong when facing temptation. The walls around our hearts ought to have gates that are in good repair and well-guarded.

It all starts with rebuilding our walls and ends with monitoring our gates, as we protect the weak and vulnerable while we also go out and serve, love, and lead others (Nehemiah 4:6, 4:13–14). Like the people in Israel who wholeheartedly joined Nehemiah in his task, I pray that you will come along on our journey toward fellowship with Jesus and meaningful service to the lost.

CHAPTER ONE

Rebuild Your Gates

And they said to me, "The remnant there in the province who had survived the exile is in great trouble and shame. The wall of Jerusalem is broken down, and its gates are destroyed by fire." As soon as I heard these words I sat down and wept and mourned for days, and I continued fasting and praying before the God of heaven.
—Nehemiah 1:3–4

We all have some damage. Whether from our own sin or the sins others have committed against us, there are parts of our souls that have been left in ruins. The brokenness of this world has left us with the need to be rebuilt by our Justifier, Jesus Christ.

Nehemiah was well acquainted with rebuilding ruins. He was in Persia, serving King Artaxerxes as his right-hand man, when he got word that his home city of Jerusalem had been attacked (Nehemiah 1:3, 2:1). The gates had been torn down, and the walls had been broken and ruined.

The damage to the temple and the city wall of Jerusalem that the Jews faced in the books of Ezra and

Nehemiah dated all the way back to the end of the divided kingdom, with the destruction of the northern kingdom of Israel and the southern kingdom of Judah. The northern kingdom fell to the Assyrians in 722 B.C., and King Shalmaneser took the people of Israel into exile in Assyria (2 Kings 18:9–12).

Subsequently, in 586 B.C., King Nebuchadnezzar of Babylon conquered Jerusalem and took the Jews into exile in Babylon. The Babylonians completely destroyed Jerusalem's city walls and the temple during their attack (Jeremiah 39:1–10). According to 2 Chronicles 36:19–20, the Babylonians "burned the house of God and broke down the wall of Jerusalem and burned all its palaces with fire and destroyed all its precious vessels. [The king] took into exile in Babylon those who had escaped from the sword, and they became servants to him and to his sons until the establishment of the kingdom of Persia." The Persian Empire began in 539 B.C., when Nabonidus, King of Babylon, surrendered to King Cyrus of Persia.

As recounted in the book of Ezra, in the first year of King Cyrus's reign, he decreed that the Jewish exiles were allowed to return home (1:1–4). At first, a group led by Zerubbabel, a man of royal blood from the line of David, and Jeshua, a priest, returned to Jerusalem and rebuilt the temple (Ezra 2–6). The next group arrived under the leadership of Ezra, a priest and a scribe, who was sent to Jerusalem to instruct the people (Ezra 7–10). Finally, Nehemiah secured permission to repair the city walls of Jerusalem, and he began his work of motivating and leading the people.

The Bible tells us that the destruction was so great, no

one could so much as enter or leave the city (Nehemiah 2:14). Nehemiah 1:3 says that the remnant in Jerusalem was "in great trouble and shame" over the destruction, and Nehemiah was so devastated over the news that, according to his own account in Scripture, he sat down and wept and mourned for days (Nehemiah 1:4).

When the entrance to your home is broken, don't you feel uneasy? When the locks don't work or the door is ajar, isn't it unsettling? Imagine trying to sleep at night, with your loved ones and those things you hold dear in your home, with the front door broken down and destroyed. I'm sure none of us would be able to sleep at all for fear that anyone could break in at any time.

Taking it a step further, how does this idea apply to the "gates" that govern our inner selves? What happens when the access points to our inner thoughts and desires are laid to waste? What happens when our defenses and fortifications have been broken down and set ablaze by sin, shame, or mistreatment by others?

Maybe the relationships within our families are damaged by mistrust and we don't believe they can be repaired. Maybe our sense of being called and valued by God is broken because we have strayed from Him and, like the prodigal son, we can't see our way back home (Luke 15:11–32). Like a once-secure home that is vulnerable because its doors are destroyed, we suddenly feel unprotected and bare when the gates of our life and our soul are in disrepair.

Brokenness Brings Healing

When made aware of the devastation of Jerusalem, Nehemiah did more than just weep and mourn for days—he also fasted and prayed before his God (Nehemiah 1:4). He wasn't willing to let the destruction stand, and from the depths of his heart, he cried out to God for direction (Nehemiah 1:5).

His recorded prayer in Nehemiah 1 starts with praise. Then his words move to repentance for the sins of his people and a request for God to give him success in the mission he felt God had laid upon him—to go help his people rebuild the walls (Nehemiah 1:5–11).

The confirmation of Nehemiah's calling came when he approached the pagan king he served and asked his permission to travel back to Jerusalem to lead the rebuilding project (Nehemiah 2:5–6). In Philippians 4:6, we are told, "in everything by prayer and supplication with thanksgiving let your requests be made known to God." Nehemiah prayed first, and then he went boldly to make his request known to the king.

In his own words, Nehemiah recounted, "The king granted me what I asked, for the good hand of my God was upon me" (Nehemiah 2:8). Not only did King Artaxerxes grant his permission, but he also sent Nehemiah with letters of permission to make his trip easier and to help him obtain building materials, as well as officers and horsemen to accompany him (Nehemiah 2:8–9).

When Nehemiah arrived in Jerusalem and saw the devastation firsthand, he realized that the ruins weren't only

physical in nature (Nehemiah 1:6–7; 2:13, 17). The Israelites, the people of God, had turned against the Lord.
Understanding their rebellion, and seeing the damage
around him, stirred something within Nehemiah.

Brokenness can move a person to action, and brokenness is often what God uses to motivate His people. It's
certainly how He motivated Nehemiah. He gathered the
official and priests and told them what God had done to
bring him to them (Nehemiah 2:16–18).

Nehemiah was so overcome by the brokenness around
him, he cried out to the people and called them back to
God, urging them to rebuild Jerusalem (Nehemiah 2:17).
And you know what? The people stepped forward. They
rose to the occasion and decided to rebuild their city, return to God, and be better than ever.

When we face the brokenness in our communities and
in our own lives, in our relationship with God and in our
relationships with others, are our hearts stirred? Are we
prompted to action?

God uses the devastation in our lives to show us our
need for Him and to cause us to act. Nehemiah felt deep
emotion about the state of Jerusalem, and even though he
was living in a foreign land, he knew he was the one God
was calling to do something about it (Nehemiah 2:4).

It took faith for Nehemiah to ask the king to release
him to return to Jerusalem, but he knew God was calling
him, so he stepped out in faith. Every step of the way, God
provided for him and guided him—proving that he was
acting in obedience.

God also provided confirmation of his calling. When

Nehemiah spoke about his vision to the Israelites, they rallied to help him with the massive rebuilding project (Nehemiah 2:18). Every step of the way, God fortified him, even when he faced opposition.

Could it be that God is calling you to act to rebuild the broken places you see before you? He gives us godly sorrow for a reason: so that He can use us to make things right. We, like Nehemiah, can be the ones God has chosen to bring wholeness to our lives, to our communities, and to our world.

All we have to do is look around us, or read the news, to realize that our culture has been subjected to the shameful ways of the world. As with Nehemiah, our collective brokenness and shame should devastate us and drive us to prayer and repentance. We are surrounded by ruins that need to be rebuilt with a renewed trust in God and a restored focus on His Word.

Living Apart from God

The book of Nehemiah is about rebuilding the city walls and rebuilding the trust between God and His people. In 2 Chronicles 15, we read about another situation where a broken relationship with God needed restoration.

This story centers on King Asa. He had come from a line of ungodly kings. The kings who preceded Asa cared more about pleasing themselves and fitting in with the culture than about pleasing God. Does that sound familiar? They worshiped idols and dishonored the ways of the Lord.

God sent a prophet to speak truth to Asa, whose heart

was tender to grasp the seriousness of the situation he had inherited (2 Chronicles 15:1–6). The Bible tells us:

> *The Spirit of God came upon Azariah the son of Oded, and he went out to meet Asa and said to him, "Hear me, Asa, and all Judah and Benjamin: The LORD is with you while you are with him. If you seek him, he will be found by you, but if you forsake him, he will forsake you."*
> **—2 Chronicles 15:1–2**

According to verse 3, Judah had been without three things for a very long time: (1) the true God, (2) a teaching priest, and (3) the Law. The lack of God, a reliable teacher, and God's Word will get you in trouble every time. Without the true God in your life, you may fall for any false god, or you may even think that *you* are god. Without a teaching priest, there is no way to learn about the true God. And without the Law or the Word of God, you end up a morally relativistic society, with everyone doing what is right in his or her own eyes.

Asa and his family had been distanced from God for many generations, yet here was God, calling Asa back to Him. As soon as Asa heard Azariah's words, he put away the pagan idols and repaired the altar of the Lord (2 Chronicles 15:8). Then he gathered the people and called them to turn back to the Lord and sacrifice to Him (2 Chronicles 15:9–10). Second Chronicles 15:12 describes their change of heart: "And they entered into a covenant to seek the LORD, the God of their fathers, with all their heart and with all their soul."

Judah was without the three things it needed to follow

God's will for the nation's future. The spiritual gates had been broken down, so to speak. The Judahites had forgotten what it was like to love and fear God, because so many kings had glorified paganism and self-worship. When Asa was finally convicted about the truth and called the people to repent, they realized they wanted to do what was right. However, they had strayed so far from the Lord that they didn't know what right behavior and faithful worship looked like. They vowed to renew their covenant, and God used Asa to restore what had been broken.

Good Is Not Right

Like the people during King Asa's time, do you find yourself trying to do good but unable to do *right?* You try to make a good choice but only make a bigger mess. Things then get worse—those first few cracks in the gate lead to full-fledged destruction, and you find that you're forced to choose to trust God or yourself.

In that moment, you must decide who you will become. Will you trust God through the turmoil and stay close to Him, repenting and boldly destroying the idols in your path as Asa did? Or will you go it your own way and move even further away from the one who wants to lead you? Will you listen to your own desires and understanding or seek the Father's wisdom for your life?

For fifteen years before Azariah came and spoke the truth to him, Asa had been trying to do what was right and serve as a good king, but he still struggled (2 Chronicles 14:2–6). He needed a word from God, through Azariah, to give him courage.

Sometimes we just need one word to believe that everything will work out—that our marriage will be restored, our children will be okay, and our communities will thrive again. We need to hear the truth from God and then act in courage, as Asa did, to tear down the idols in our lives and rebuild our relationship with the one true God. Because of Asa's faithfulness, the people returned to God and the land had peace for thirty-five years.

It's Time to Rebuild Your Wall

God spoke to Nehemiah, and his life was changed. The same thing happened for Asa, Gideon, Samuel, David, Peter, and so many others in the Bible. These stories of God imparting courage to His followers and changing their lives aren't merely out-of-date accounts of history—they are reminders for you today, as well.

You can be the next person who hears from God, turns to Him, and sees idols fall and walls restored. When God tells you it's time to rebuild your wall, tear down your idols, and form a covenant with Him, do it! The change may not happen overnight, and you may get discouraged, but if you keep trusting in your relationship with God, He will strengthen you.

Surround yourself with people who believe in your calling, as Nehemiah did. Find courage from God and from the people around you, as Asa did. Remove the things in your life that are keeping you from the Lord, and ask God to show you how to rebuild the ruined places.

Like the Judahites who repented with Asa, promise to seek the Lord with all of your heart and all of your soul, and believe that He will give you the courage for the task before you. Just as He did with all of the people He used to change hearts and bring about His victory in the Bible, He is ready to use you to lead a mighty rebuilding project.

WORKBOOK

Chapter One Questions

Question: What was the physical significance of the broken walls around Jerusalem? What was the spiritual parallel for the Jews?

_____

_____

_____

_____

_____

_____

_____

_____

_____

_____

_____

Question: What three things was Judah without in the days of Asa? What was the impact of lacking these things?

_____

_____

_____

_____

_____

_____

_____

_____

_____

_____

_____

_____

Question: *Good is not right.* Describe a time when your action appeared good, or you did the best you could, but it was not truly *right*.

_____

_____

_____

_____

_____

_____

_____

_____

_____

_____

_____

Action: What is an area of sorrow and/or brokenness in your life? How could God use your burden to guide and direct your life and to help you bring restoration to yourself or others?

Chapter One Notes

_____

_____

_____

_____

_____

_____

_____

_____

_____

_____

_____

_____

_____

_____

_____

_____

_____

_____

_____

_____

_____

_____

_____

_____

CHAPTER TWO

A Firm Foundation

But be doers of the word, and not hearers only, deceiving yourselves. For if anyone is a hearer of the word and not a doer, he is like a man who looks intently at his natural face in a mirror. For he looks at himself and goes away and at once forgets what he was like. But the one who looks into the perfect law, the law of liberty, and perseveres, being no hearer who forgets but a doer who acts, he will be blessed in his doing.

—James 1:22–25

A well-known Persian proverb says, "Thinking well is wise, planning well is wiser, doing well wisest and best of all."

We all know people who can quote hundreds of Bible verses from memory, but that knowledge alone isn't enough. The Bible reminds us that we must be doers of the Word, not only hearers (James 1:22). We must build our foundation through the head knowledge and the heart knowledge gained from acting on the truth (James 1:25).

We can gain understanding through our experiences,

but misinterpretation of our experiences can lead us astray. We may also rely on mentors or teachers, but even those who seem to have the right answers may not speak truth to us.

The best way to get head and heart knowledge—the best way to grow in your faith and in the Lord, in other words—is through knowing and applying the Word of God, staying plugged in to the church, and learning more about following Christ from leaders of the faith. Romans 10:17 says that "faith comes from hearing and hearing through the Word of God."

God has given us two very important tools on our journey: His Word and the church. If we are serious about pursuing spiritual maturity, we will invest deeply in both of these resources.

Growing deeper in our faith is a journey that will never truly end until we reach heaven. This learning helps strengthen our spiritual walls. It gives us both protection from the enemy's plans and the stamina to keep running the race. As Paul wrote in Philippians 3:13–14: "Brothers, I do not consider that I have made it my own. But one thing I do: forgetting what lies behind and straining forward to what lies ahead, I press on toward the goal for the prize of the upward call of God in Christ Jesus."

If we are continuing to study God's Word and seek wisdom from godly teachers, we will find ourselves becoming more mature and our foundation getting stronger. As we press forward in our journeys, we never stop learning, and we never stop maturing until the day of Christ comes (Philippians 1:6).

Giving, Not Getting

How do we know if we need to sharpen our head and heart knowledge? One indication is when we have a "Savior-only" mindset. This happens when God is our Savior and *only* our Savior. We want Him to save us from the bills, from adversity, from our neighbors, from our coworkers, from sickness, from all the trials and difficult circumstances of life. When Almighty God is reduced to spiritual Santa Claus, we forget that our Heavenly Father desires to have an authentic, growing relationship with His children.

When we limit God to being only our Savior, we choose to operate in an immature, child-like mindset. Babies cry because they either want or need something. As their parents, we immediately step in to respond because they aren't yet mature enough to assess whether the need is actual or perceived, let alone address true needs on their own.

At a certain point, however, as the child grows, we parents adjust our response in order to create a space for learning to take place. We facilitate the maturation process by allowing our children to learn self-discipline, to solve problems, and to operate in the security of what they know to be true. What our children should know to be true is that, as their parents, we will either provide or give them access to everything they need to succeed in this life.

By contrast, parents who give their children everything and step in to save their children from every conflict, minor or major, real or perceived, are labeled irresponsible.

One thing we know is that God is not an irresponsible parent! He has truly provided everything that we need to succeed in this life and the life to come, including opportunities to know Him and the power to overcome (2 Peter 1:3).

Choosing a limited, Savior-only approach to God only inhibits our relationship with the Father, hinders the work of the Holy Spirit, and keeps us from growing up into Christ. We will not grow into spiritual maturity if we continue to act like babies, always expecting to receive while barely giving.

If you feel like your spiritual walls are weak and crumbling, it may be because you are only going to God when you are in a crisis:

"My spiritual walls are in rough shape." *(Problem)*

"I know of this amazing bricklayer who could do a fantastic job rebuilding my wall." *(Solution)*

"This information only benefits me if I know the bricklayer's phone number and trust the bricklayer enough to actually call and secure His help." *(Condition)*

Like a house, your relationship with God requires preventative maintenance in order to function at its best as intended. Don't wait until the walls start to collapse and the roof caves in!

With this in mind, seek to grow in Christ. As you mature in the faith, you will find yourself being strengthened through a renewed relationship with your Heavenly Father.

As babies grow up into adolescence and then adulthood, they learn that the richness in relationships has less to do with what they can get and more with what they can give. Likewise, as we mature and become secure in what God has already done in Christ, we seek to respond out of loving gratitude—to give, not get. We discover that joy and true connection are found when we start giving ourselves away.

What resources or talents do you have that you are keeping to yourself? How might the Kingdom of God be enriched if you were to step out of your comfort zone and give of yourself so that others may experience God's love? And how might the act of giving yourself away deepen your relationship with the God who gave you those resources and talents in the first place?

Our model in this way of life is the Lord Himself. In the first scripture most of us ever learned, we hear that "God so loved the world, that he *gave* his only Son" (John 3:16, emphasis added). In Matthew 20:28, Jesus made His own mission clear when He said that "the Son of Man came not to be served but to serve, and to give his life as a ransom for many."

Jesus showed His followers what a true servant's lifestyle looked like, in vivid color, when He washed His disciples' feet before the Last Supper. They were told, as are we, that they should go and do the same for others.

Are you relying on your head knowledge alone but failing to put it into action? When we give ourselves away for God's glory, we find true joy and purpose. Those people who think they are doing something for His glory when in reality they're just standing still are blowing in the wind. They stand on an unsteady foundation, and their house is likely to collapse around them when tough times arrive and their faith is tested (Matthew 7:24–27).

Know Jesus

An entire industry of pop culture media, from *People* magazine to the *National Enquirer* to *Entertainment Tonight*, is built on the idea that people want to know every little detail about celebrities. You can read all the articles you want about a famous actor or a star quarterback, but that is very different from actually *knowing* that person.

You may know what kind of pie your favorite pop singer likes the best. You may even know details about his or her family. But if you ran into that singer on the street, , he or she would not have the first clue who you are.

Unfortunately, some who profess to follow Christ are in the same predicament. They know plenty *about* Jesus, but they don't truly *know* Him. You might have read the Bible every day and learned everything there is to know about the life of Christ, but something would be missing.

Imagine being married to someone who believed that the way to intimacy was only by learning *about* you. You would crave for your heart to be truly known, because that's how we truly connect with each other.

The difference between knowing about Jesus and truly knowing Jesus is laid out by John:

Whoever says "I know him" but does not keep his com-
mandments is a liar, and the truth is not in him, but
whoever keeps his word, in him truly the love of God is per-
fected. By this we may know that we are in him: whoever
says he abides in him ought to walk in the same way in
which he walked.

—1 John 2:4–6

John's letter goes on to clarify that if we truly want to claim to abide in Christ, we must walk through our lives in the same way Jesus walked. How do we prove that we know Jesus? By keeping His commandments and walking in His ways.

Bear Fruit

As we seek to live out our faith with both head knowledge and heart knowledge, growing every day in our knowing Christ as He knows us, we show a deepening relationship by bearing spiritual fruit. The Bible is very clear that the fruit of the Spirit serves as evidence that a follower of Christ is truly obeying His Word and walking in His steps.

But the fruit of the Spirit is love, joy, peace, patience, kind-
ness, goodness, faithfulness, gentleness, self-control;
against such things there is no law.

—Galatians 5:22–23

If we are becoming more like Christ every day, our lives will naturally display these spiritual fruits.

Displaying the fruit of the Spirit means that we will be

in the process of becoming more loving, more joyful, and more patient each day, with the Holy Spirit's help. Maturing in Christ is a process, but if you are truly trusting the Lord, others *around* you should be able to see the change *in* you.

We should always be improving to be more Christlike, and we should always strive to fulfill our destiny. The only way to accomplish living in Christ and for Christ is to be faithful in all things and to live a life worthy of the calling.

Of course, we are human, and we still struggle with sin, so even as we are maturing and showing the fruit of the Spirit, we will inevitably stumble. When we stumble, just like a baby learning to walk, we let our Father help us up and we start again. If our goal is to become mature in Christ, we need to fight for it—even when our sinful nature and the Devil threaten to pull us down.

Later in Galatians 5:25, after he lists the fruit of the Spirit, Paul encourages us this way: "If we live by the Spirit, let us also walk by the Spirit" (NASB). If you are a follower of Jesus, you have received the Holy Spirit. The Spirit will give you the strength to walk with the Lord and live a spiritually fruitful life. Even when you trip and fall, you have everything you need to get back up and grow to maturity in Christ.

You can measure how fully your life is yielded to God by looking down that list of fruit of the Spirit and checking off the ones you show consistently. Ask your closest friends and family members which ones they see in you. We all have areas we need to surrender to the Lord, but

He is the source of strength we need to become more fruitful in our walk with Him. Remember, we cannot overcome and bear much fruit in our own strength!

Do Not Be Discouraged

We all have areas where we struggle, and we all need encouragement and support to keep our eyes on the Lord. The best place to work toward maturation in Christ is church, but in our culture today, the importance of church is being downplayed. The time we spend together in the body of Christ seems to be less important than other Sunday activities. However, in reality, nothing is more important than coming together and strengthening one another as we worship the Lord. So, when you come to church, come alert and ready to receive what the Lord has to teach you!

God made us to thrive in community and to be replenished in fellowship—to need each other. Imagine trying to rebuild a brick wall on your own. You can't do it nearly as well, or as quickly, without help. If I have to do it all myself—design the wall, lay the foundation, make the bricks, prep the mortar, lay the brick, and so forth—my wall is doomed. But our wise Heavenly Father designed us each to have different strengths that work in harmony together.

Note that we all have different strengths and are at different points on our path toward spiritual maturity. Don't be surprised or frustrated when you encounter people who are supposed to be believers yet still act like babies spiritually. Some people aren't able to receive and act on the

Word of truth—they are like the ones the Bible says are tossed by the wind, led astray by the world or their own desires (Ephesians 4:14).

When you see babes in Christ who refuse to seek maturity, keep running your own race, looking to gain head knowledge and heart knowledge as you learn from the Word of God and through His church. God promises to strengthen you if you keep your eyes on Him and refuse to let discouragement pull you down.

There is a story about the Devil having a yard sale. He put all his tools up for sale: the tools of envy, pride, deceit, and so on. There was a worn-out tool that was separated from the others, and it had a very high price tag. When asked why, the Devil replied, "This is my tool of discouragement. It's much more useful than the others. I can get into a man's heart much more easily with this tool than with any of my other tricks, because so few people know that it belongs to me."[1]

Do not become discouraged if your foundation isn't as solid as it should be. Do not let the Devil get that foothold! Instead, understand that maturity is a constant pursuit. It is living every single day, striving to grow in Christ. When you see a fellow believer conquer an old sin or habit, or you witness a brother or sister showing the fruit of the Spirit, encourage that person and build him or her up. The Bible makes it clear that we mourn with those who mourn and celebrate with those who celebrate, because we are one body in Christ (Romans 12:15).

Are you looking for opportunities to grow in Christ and to encourage those around you who want to follow Him more closely? Examine your mindset daily. Get into the

Word of God daily. Ask Him to give you strength to stand against the things that threaten to knock you down. Look for opportunities to grow in Him in the midst of your ordinary daily circumstances.

If your heart is truly seeking Him, He will honor your desire by helping you repair the walls of your heart—so that they become stronger than ever before.

Chapter Two Questions

Question: What are the two main tools God has given us to build up our foundation?

_____

_____

_____

_____

_____

_____

_____

_____

_____

_____

Question: What is the danger of viewing Jesus as Savior only? How can a person move from knowing *about* Jesus to *knowing* Him?

_____

_____

_____

_____

_____

_____

_____

_____

_____

_____

_____

Question: Read again the list of the fruits of the Spirit. How have you grown in these qualities since becoming a Christian? What are the areas that still need improvement?

_____

_____

_____

_____

_____

_____

_____

_____

_____

_____

_____

Action: Think of someone you know who is battling discouragement. Take time to write them a note, send them a text, or make a call to offer biblically-based encouragement.

Chapter Two Notes

_____

_____

_____

_____

_____

_____

_____

_____

_____

_____

_____

_____

_____

_____

_____

_____

_____

_____

_____

_____

_____

CHAPTER THREE

Courage in the Lord

Then Mordecai told them to reply to Esther, "Do not think to yourself that in the king's palace you will escape any more than all the other Jews. For if you keep silent at this time, relief and deliverance will rise for the Jews from another place, but you and your father's house will perish. And who knows whether you have not come to the kingdom for such a time as this?" Then Esther told them to reply to Mordecai, "Go, gather all the Jews to be found in Susa, and hold a fast on my behalf, and do not eat or drink for three days, night or day. I and my young women will also fast as you do. Then I will go to the king, though it is against the law, and if I perish, I perish."
—Esther 4:13–16

Would you be willing to lay down your life if you knew it would save countless others' lives? Can you imagine the fear and trembling that would accompany weighing such a decision? Would you have the courage to do the right thing even if you knew it would cost you everything? Esther is an example of such courage. And this same courage is available for all of us in Christ.

In the book of Esther, we read about King Ahasuerus, a Persian king who was unhappy in his marriage (Esther 1:12). They were a pagan people, so he sent the queen away and began to search for a new wife (Esther 1:19). He sent a message out to 170 provinces, from India to Ethiopia, looking for virgins who would make suitable queens (Esther 2:2). He put them through a yearlong audition process, and in the end, he selected a young lady from the capital city of Shushan, whose name was Esther (Esther 2:17).

Esther quickly became a favorite of the king. Soon after she assumed her new role, she learned something disturbing from her uncle Mordecai, who was also working for the king. Mordecai told Esther that one of the king's ministers, Haman, had it in for the Jewish people and was planning to put all Jews to death because they would not bow to the Persian king (Esther 4:1–9).

What was the problem? Esther and Mordecai were Jewish.

The king did not know that Esther was a Jew, so she had a choice: she could reveal the truth and ask that her people be spared, or she could say nothing and save herself from probable death.

She chose to be courageous. Esther asked to approach the king even though she had not been invited to address him, an act which was also punishable by death (Esther 4:15–16). But Esther knew she had been put in her position so that she could save her people (Esther 4:14).

Because of Esther's boldness and Mordecai's encouragement, the Jews were spared and Haman, who had hatched the plot, was punished. The heart of the book of

Esther is found in Esther 4:14, when Mordecai challenges her:

> *For if you keep silent at this time, relief and deliverance will rise for the Jews from another place, but you and your father's house will perish. And who knows whether you have not come to the kingdom for such a time as this?*

Just like Esther, we are undercover. We are positioned to do great things for God—so much that it may scare us at times. We may be afraid at the thought of being bold for Christ, yet we must choose: Will we step out in our faith? Or will we shrink back and disappear in the shadows, missing the opportunity to be used by God in a mighty way?

You may look at the walls crumbling around your heart and feel that you have nothing left to give. Standing boldly can make our lives more difficult than we ever imagined. Perhaps you acted courageously in the past and had to bear the brunt of a spiritual attack.

Be encouraged! God has not left you alone. Even if you are tired and battered, He is with you. He will give you the strength you need to get through whatever He calls you to do. He will repair the damage to your spiritual walls if you let Him.

No Time for Naysayers

There will always be someone who doesn't understand you and the calling God has placed on your life. There will always be someone who is jealous of what you have.

There will always be someone competing against you. There will always be someone trying to trip you up.

If we understand that we are destined to bring God glory and that He has given us special gifts, we will be confident to do His work even when those around us want to erode that confidence by making us doubt ourselves.

Like Esther, we all feel fear sometimes, especially when God is calling us to take a risk. Our fear can paralyze us and numb us. What if we fail? What if we slip up? What if we look like fools? What if we lose friends, status, or respect?

In the moments when fear threatens to overwhelm us, we need to lean on the truths of God's Word and surround ourselves with people who will encourage us, as Mordecai did for Esther. Other believers will often confirm God's Word to us—that we have been called to the place where we are "for such a time as this," to fulfill God's purpose, which is much greater than our own purposes (Esther 4:14).

We may not always acknowledge His calling, because of our fear, but everybody encounters fear. The only difference between a brave person and a fearful person is that a brave person fights through fear. You must fight through it with the confidence that God's Word and His promises are true, understanding that His love and faithfulness are greater than any negative messages from the world.

When fear invades our thoughts, it's easy to try to tell God how and when to use you: *"Okay, God, use me here, but don't use me there because my friends are there and they will see me. They will think I'm crazy."* But I am here to tell you that we cannot dictate when and how God wants to use us any more than we can dictate His calling on our lives. Don't you think Esther wished she had never been made queen—that she could have stayed in her quiet life as a Jewish girl being raised by her uncle?

But God had a higher calling. He called her to be a bridge between His will and the world, and He is calling many of us to be bridges as well. Remember that He doesn't put you into a job, a family, or a neighborhood by accident. He has a plan to use His people if they fight through their fear and step into His plan courageously.

We Are Called

At first, Esther thought she could hide, and sometimes we may feel the same way. We hide at home and at church, in our cubicle and in our schedules. We hide within our Christian communities. God reveals our gifts to others, and we are presented with opportunities to use those gifts, yet we decline because of our fear. We shrug off the opportunity. But if we hide from God's calling, we miss the chance to be used by Him in mighty ways.

Imagine what would have happened if Esther had hidden in her royal chambers, comfortably being waited on by servants, surrounded by luxury, and ignoring the reality of the plot against her people. The consequences to the Jewish people might have been disastrous, and we would not have Esther's example of faithfulness today.

One of the primary ways we hide today is by surrounding ourselves with other believers. It feels safe and comfortable, but all the while, we're hiding from God. Staying in our "holy huddle" feels easier than stepping out into the places where God has called us to do His work. We stay in church or Bible study, avoiding the gifts and the opportunities God has placed before us and hoping that maybe He will give our calling to someone else.

In John 17, near the end of His life, Jesus prayed a long and heartfelt prayer for us—for the believers meant to carry His Word to the world following His ascent to heaven. He didn't ask God to put us behind church walls and lock us in there, or to create worlds where we are only around other Christians.

Instead, Jesus prayed that we would be sent out into the world so that "the world may know that you sent me and loved them even as you loved me" (John 17:23). The Bible says that we are the vessels God wants to use (2 Corinthians 4:7). We just need to be bold enough to step out with courage and dare to do what God wants us to do. As we step out in faith, He will give us the strength and the gifts to take the next step—and the next.

Comfort-Zone Christianity

Esther had it pretty good. She was a queen, living in a palace. She had all her needs met, yet God asked something very brave of her. She could have said no, but instead, she chose courage. She took a risk for her people, and she saved them all.

We are not so different.

We live good lives here in the United States. Our needs are met; we have freedom of religion and of speech. And all God wants us to do is be brave and stand up for Him— to use our talents and rise to the occasion. God wants us to step away from our comfortable places and go to places where people don't know the great love of God and haven't seen bold demonstrations of faith.

We get too comfortable—we don't appreciate all that God has given us, and we fail to look for the ways we can reach out to the people in the world who face very real struggles.

You have plenty to eat but may feel sorry for yourself because you can't afford to go out to a fancy restaurant, while people elsewhere in the world feel blessed to have one meal a day.

You may have a shelf full of Bibles, and you can go to church several times a week. But in some countries, believers are trying to figure out ways to disguise their Bibles so that they can smuggle them to people who may not have the opportunity ever to read the Word of God if believers didn't take the risk.

If God is giving you a burden for people who are in need, or those who are persecuted for their faith, don't you dare let that calling pass you by!

Romans 12 says that He's given us different gifts and callings (Romans 12:4–8). Some of us are prophets, some of us are ministers, some of us are gifted with exhortation, and some of us are gifted with teaching. Some of us have mercy; some of us have diligence. Some have creativity and singing and dancing. Some have skills in negotiating or writing.

You need to ask God to show you what your gifts are and then work each gift for His glory. Use it any chance you get! You are a gift to God's kingdom when you are willing and available to be used to do His work with the gifts He has given you. You are uniquely gifted, and God wants to use the gift He gave you.

Luke 12 says that to whom much is given, much is required (Luke 12:48). Paul wrote in Romans 11:29 that the gifts and the callings of God are irrevocable—they are real and can't be taken away from you. Your destiny isn't going anywhere. You have your assignments, according to your gifts and calling, and I have mine.

No one but Esther could have taken the assignment she was given, so it was crucial for her to obey and live into it. When we follow and serve God, we are rewarded by the knowledge that we are helping build His kingdom. So, why not live up to the challenge? Your individual call to do God's work is waiting for you!

Choose to Be Bold

In the midst of our fear and worries, *we press on.* We choose to be bold. We choose to use our gifts and to accept our callings. Esther was certainly fearful, but she knew it was her time. In Esther 4:16, she sent a message to Mordecai and told him, "If I perish, I perish." She boldly stepped in and embraced her assignment, and countless lives were saved as a result. Our circumstances may not be as dramatic as hers, but God is calling us to do the same.

And that, my friends, is courage. God has placed courage within us. He desires to bless you as you respond courageously to His call and seek opportunities to use your gifts to advance the Kingdom of God.

When I think back to Nehemiah, I imagine the panic he

felt when he heard about the state of the walls around Jerusalem. His ancestors had already been conquered and carried off. Now, anyone could come in and further ransack the city. The Jews were surely living in hope that God would return them to the Promised Land. What state would it be in when they returned?

Similarly, I worry at the state of the walls that many Christians have around their hearts. These walls have been neglected for so long that it won't take much before they aren't able to keep out the enemy, never mind having to stand up and do something truly courageous.

You may not feel that you're being called to do something bold. Regardless, now is the time for you to build up the walls around your heart—so that you're ready to stand strong when God calls you to help save countless lives in the world around you.

Chapter Three Questions

Question: In what ways did Esther model courage? What can you learn from her example?

_____

_____

_____

_____

_____

_____

_____

_____

_____

_____

_____

_____

Question: When has fear kept you from obeying God's call? Who are some "Mordecais" in your life who have helped confirm God's plan for you?

_____

_____

_____

_____

_____

_____

_____

_____

_____

_____

_____

_____

Question: What is your personal comfort zone? When are you tempted to hide there instead of following God's call?

_____

_____

_____

_____

_____

_____

_____

_____

_____

_____

_____

_____

Action: What is your "such a time as this"? Think of one courageous act outside of your comfort zone that God is leading you to undertake at this time. Ask two or three Christian friends to pray for you as you obediently step forward to answer God's call.

Chapter Three Notes

_____

_____

_____

_____

_____

_____

_____

_____

_____

_____

_____

_____

_____

_____

_____

_____

_____

_____

_____

_____

_____

_____

_____

_____

CHAPTER FOUR

Hold Your Ground Against the Enemy

But that is not the way you learned Christ!—assuming that you have heard about him and were taught in him, as the truth is in Jesus, to put off your old self, which belongs to your former manner of life and is corrupt through deceitful desires, and to be renewed in the spirit of your minds, and to put on the new self, created after the likeness of God in true righteousness and holiness. Therefore, having put away falsehood, let each one of you speak the truth with his neighbor, for we are members one of another. Be angry and do not sin; do not let the sun go down on your anger and give no opportunity to the devil.
—Ephesians 4:20–27

My friend, you are not the person you used to be. You have access to a much better life, but you must put away the old habits and adopt the new. You must rebuild your gates with the truth of Christ. In Ephesians, we learn that we can be renewed in our minds. Because of Christ, we each have a new self, created after the likeness of God. We have so much freedom because of our new self!

We don't have to be slaves to sin anymore (Romans 6:6), but Paul goes on to warn us in Ephesians 4 about giving the Devil a foothold. If we let anger rule us—if we go to sleep while we are angry, dwelling on bitterness and past sins—we throw the door open for the Devil to move into our lives. It is the Devil's goal to rob us of the freedom we are meant to have in Christ. This battle is very real, but when we follow and submit to Christ, we are assured of victory.

The Roaring Lion

When we chase anger, jealousy, and pride, we give the Devil a foothold in our lives. He is the accuser before God. He is the tempter; he is the one who hinders our plans. He is real, not fiction. The Bible says he is the spirit that attacks the righteous. He made his first big impact in the Garden of Eden in Genesis 3, and he's been after us ever since.

Creators of television shows and movies love to tell stories about the Devil and satanic forces, stories designed to scare people but not to teach the truth about who the Devil really is. We watch these fictional accounts and love the horror, but through Hollywood's influence, we have been desensitized to the reality of evil forces battling with the Holy Spirit in our lives. When we ignore the Devil as he encourages us to sin, we give him a foothold.

We're used to imagining that the enemy will come for us in big, scary ways. On the contrary, the Devil doesn't need to do something huge when he can use clever tactics. He won't come at your walls with a battering ram. Instead, he'll convince you to dismantle the wall on your own, brick by brick. We must be ever vigilant against this crafty opponent.

We learn more about the Devil in Ezekiel 28. There, we read a prophecy against the evil king of Tyre. However, we know that it is actually a dual prophecy, likening the evil king to Satan. In Ezekiel 28:8, we read, "They shall thrust you down into the pit, and you shall die the death of the slain in the heart of the seas." The Word of God is clear that Satan will not get the ultimate victory. In verse 14, the prophecy calls the Devil an "anointed guardian cherub," reminding us that the Devil once had a lofty position above the angels.

In the book of Job, we learn that the Devil loves to test us. He loves to mess with us. He saw that Job was a righteous man, so he asked God for permission to persecute Job, hoping that the man of God would forsake his faith (Job 1:8–12). (Notice that the Devil can't do anything without God's permission!)

The Devil will come along and try to test you, but if you have the Holy Spirit and are living your life as a follower of Christ, you will ultimately pass the test. But don't be surprised when the trials and tests come, because the Devil is anxiously looking for an opportunity to attack, just as he was prowling around Job (1 Peter 5:8).

In 1 John 3:8, we learn that sin and the love of sin comes from the Devil. We all trip and mess up sometimes, but we need to realize that when we desire to sin, we are listening to the Devil, not the Lord. The Devil loves to try to convince us that our sinful choices aren't really destructive—that just a little bit of sin is fine. But whenever we follow the sinful flesh, it pulls us away from the Lord and His plan for our lives.

Pay close attention to Peter's warning:

> *Humble yourselves, therefore, under the mighty hand of God so that at the proper time he may exalt you, casting all your anxieties on him, because he cares for you. Be sober-minded; be watchful. Your adversary the devil prowls around like a roaring lion, seeking someone to devour.*
> **—1 Peter 5:6–8**

The Devil isn't playing around. He wants to devour us! He is always trying to tempt us—to entice us out of our safe place with God.

In Ephesians 6, we learn about the spiritual warfare going on all around us:

> *Finally, be strong in the Lord and in the strength of his might. Put on the whole armor of God, that you may be able to stand against the schemes of the devil. For we do not wrestle against flesh and blood, but against the rulers, against the authorities, against the cosmic powers over this present darkness, against the spiritual forces of evil in the heavenly places. Therefore take up the whole armor of God, that you may be able to withstand in the evil day, and having done all, to stand firm.*
> **—Ephesians 6:10–13**

The attacks we face come from the spiritual realm, and later in Ephesians, we are given assurance of our spiritual armor—the weapons God gives us to defend ourselves against Satan's attacks. Because we have trusted in Christ, we have the belt of truth, the breastplate of righteousness, the shoes of the gospel of peace, the shield of faith, the helmet of salvation, and the sword of the Spirit (Ephesians 6:14–18).

Satan and his minions never stop their attack. Once our defenses are lowered, they move in. And the fact is, we can't fight them off ourselves. We need help.

Our Battle Armor

Help comes in the form of the armor of God, as described in Ephesians. God in His faithfulness has equipped us to combat the threats and strategies of the Devil. But it's not merely about saying, "I'm putting on my breastplate of righteousness" (Ephesians 4:14). Don't just get up in the morning and tell yourself, "I'm strapping on my shield of faith," or "I'm picking up the sword of the Spirit" (Ephesians 4:16–17), and then forget about it, getting caught up in everyday life. Rather, we must adopt a new lifestyle.

We live with the Spirit of God inside of us. When we soak ourselves in the Word, we have the truth in our hearts. Prayer keeps us focused. This is what protects you and me. It's much more than simply saying that we're going to put on our armor. We have protection from the roaring lion when we commit ourselves to living our lives with Christ front and center.

When we are close with God—reading His Word, praying daily, and listening to His Spirit—we don't need to run from the Devil's tricks and schemes. No weapon formed against us will prosper (Isaiah 54:17 NASB) when we trust wholeheartedly in the promises of Jesus. We must stay put. We must stand our ground (Ephesians 6:14).

The Devil will try to find a seat at your table. He will try to infiltrate your family, your soul, and your calling. Do not give him room. Kick him out! In the name of Jesus, you don't have to put up with him.

You were meant to lead your family; *you* were meant to have a legacy of godliness; *you* were meant to stand for the salvation of the Lord. It's a matter of authority, and if we are one with Christ, *we* have the authority because of the Lord Almighty. The Devil may try to convince you that he has power in your life, but he actually has nothing if you don't give him a foothold.

When you stay firm in God's promises—when you stay true to His truth—the Devil won't get his foothold. You will be free to live by the Spirit and see the Kingdom prevail in your family, in your workplace, in your community, and in your ministry.

Hold Your Ground

In Africa, when antelopes are born, their mothers are their main form of defense to protect the babies from lions. But the mom can't stay nearby all day, and when she goes off to graze, the baby's only hope is to stay in the tall grass. The lions know the baby antelopes are in the area, so they are always searching—looking for the ones they wish to devour. The only hope is for the babies to stay down and not move an inch.

In the lions' search for these baby antelopes, they call out and roar to create fear in the hearts of the baby antelopes. The fear builds and builds.

Some baby antelopes stay put. They hide in the grass and they are safe. But some let the fear get to them. They are deceived into thinking that running away is their best option. So they start to move, and that's when it's all over. They've betrayed their location to the lion, whose very intention was to devour them (1 Peter 5:8).

Stay in your spot, my friend! Do not give the Devil a place at your table. Hold your ground and stay in the place where God has put you—where He has told you to plant yourself and serve Him. If you are planted firmly in God's will, the Devil cannot flush you out.

Stand firm. Hold on to the truth and allow the Holy Spirit to strengthen your spiritual armor so that the walls guarding your heart stand firm against the enemy's attacks.

Chapter Four Questions

Question: Contrast the cultural view of the Devil with what the Bible teaches.

_____

_____

_____

_____

_____

_____

_____

_____

_____

_____

_____

Question: What does it mean to put on your spiritual armor? How can you make this a lifestyle instead of a ritual?

_____

_____

_____

_____

_____

_____

_____

_____

_____

_____

_____

Question: Is there a place in your life in which you are wavering and Satan is attacking? What will you do to hold your ground?

_____

_____

_____

_____

_____

_____

_____

_____

_____

_____

_____

_____

Action: Memorize Ephesians 6:10–18. What does each piece of your armor teach you about the kind of battle-ready life you should be living?

Chapter Four Notes

CHAPTER FIVE

The Truth Will Set You Free

So Jesus said to the Jews who had believed him, "If you abide in my word, you are truly my disciples, and you will know the truth, and the truth will set you free." They answered him, "We are offspring of Abraham and have never been enslaved to anyone. How is it that you say, 'You will become free'?"

Jesus answered them, "Truly, truly, I say to you, everyone who practices sin is a slave to sin. The slave does not remain in the house forever; the son remains forever. So if the Son sets you free, you will be free indeed.
—John 8:31–36

Everyone wants to be free. We want to walk in the liberty that comes from having all our burdens lifted. We want to dance in the knowledge that we are loved and redeemed, cleansed from all our sin. The good news is, we can be free. Freedom has been purchased and made fully available to us.

Not only will the truth of Christ protect us from Satan, but according to John 8:32, the truth will also set us free.

In this passage, Jesus was instructing a group of Jews and telling them that abiding by His Word, as students of His Word, would set them free. This was great news, because in the age of the Pharisees and Sadducees, Jewish people were told they had to obey countless rules and customs to be right with God. When Jesus came, He criticized that way of thinking and showed them a new path to freedom.

Yet the people had trouble grasping what Jesus was saying, because they didn't see that they were truly enslaved to the old Jewish law and their many rules and expectations. In John 8:33, they responded to Jesus with this question: "We are offspring of Abraham and have never been enslaved to anyone. How is it that you say, 'You will become free?'"

False Freedom

Just like with the response to Jesus in verse 33, there are always people who believe they are already free. They think they have the truth because they read a lot or have a few educational degrees. Or the world may tell them they're free because they have reached a certain age or because they have a good job and can take care of their families. But anything can enslave us, even good things like family and jobs. Unless we put our faith in Christ, we will spend our lives being bound to the idols of this world.

If then you have been raised with Christ, seek the things that are above, where Christ is, seated at the right hand of God. Set your minds on things that are above, not on things that are on earth. For you have died, and your life is hidden with Christ in God. When Christ who is your life appears, then you also will appear with him in glory. Put to death therefore what is earthly in you: sexual immorality, impurity, passion, evil desire, and covetousness, which is idolatry.

—Colossians 3:1–5

According to the standards of the world today, it's more about how much money you have than how rich you are in Christ. We can also get caught up in the lie that when we know a lot *about* the truth, we actually *know* the truth.

But the reality is this: only by knowing and following the truth of Jesus can you truly be free. And isn't freedom the thing we crave the most? God created us to seek freedom, and He is the only authentic source for it: "Now the Lord is the Spirit, and where the Spirit of the Lord is, there is freedom" (2 Corinthians 3:17).

You aren't free simply because you know the right people or because you're related to so-and-so. You're not free just because you're friends with the pastor. You're not even free because you go to church every time they open the doors, give money, or sing in the choir.

And even if our gospel is veiled, it is veiled to those who are perishing. In their case the god of this world has blinded the minds of the unbelievers, to keep them from seeing the light of the gospel of the glory of Christ, who is the image of God.

—2 Corinthians 4:3–4

The god of this world, Satan, has veiled or blinded the

minds of those who are perishing. We were all once perishing. Unless the light of the gospel shines upon the perishing, we will remain blind, unable to turn and find truth. Do you see? Truth comes through Christ, and faith in Christ is the only path to true freedom.

Slaves to Sin

Jesus made it crystal clear when He said, "Truly, truly, I say to you, everyone who practices sin is a slave to sin" (John 8:34). The thing about slavery is, you can't wake up one day and just decide not to be a slave. It doesn't work that way. When you are in bondage, you may crave freedom, but those chains are too strong for you to loosen on your own strength.

I see so many people trying to get out of sin slavery on their own. They try to do the right things and read the right books and listen to the right speakers. But the Devil's not going to let you off the hook just because you want him to. You may think you have found a way to freedom—and for a short while, you may feel free—but ultimately, you will just move onto a different type of bondage if Christ isn't on the throne of your life. When you face enough pressure, you will revert back to that life of slavery to sin.

This realization should make us even more determined to share the gospel with the people around us. We hold the key to their freedom! You may know people who look like they have it all together, but if they aren't walking with Christ, they are living in bondage and need you to introduce them to the Savior who offers freedom.

So then, brothers, we are debtors, not to the flesh, to live according to the flesh. For if you live according to the flesh you will die, but if by the Spirit you put to death the deeds of the body, you will live. For all who are led by the Spirit of God are sons of God. For you did not receive the spirit of slavery to fall back into fear, but you have received the Spirit of adoption as sons, by whom we cry, "Abba! Father!" The Spirit himself bears witness with our spirit that we are children of God, and if children, then heirs—heirs of God and fellow heirs with Christ, provided we suffer with him in order that we may also be glorified with him.
—Romans 8:12–17

Freedom in Christ is a funny thing, because it requires us to surrender. There is only one way to cross from this life to the next, and that is to die. There is only one way to grow a tree, and that is to plant a seed. There is only one way that the sun rises in the morning and sets in the evening, and that's from the rotation of the earth. Everything has to have a beginning, a foundation, and that's who God is in this world.

There is only *one* way to get free: through a commitment to following Jesus. We will live into our freedom in Christ by worshiping God as a lifestyle, submitting to live by His Word, and serving others. In doing so, we will make our churches safe places for those who are enslaved to sin to come and find freedom.

Don't allow your church to become a country club for religious people. Every one of us, even those who were raised in the church, struggles with sin, and we need to create spaces where we can share our brokenness and truly support each other even when trials come.

Sin is the number one danger to our spiritual walls.

Whether it's our sin, the sin of others, or the sin of the world, it tears down our walls faster than anything else. You may feel that your walls are too damaged to be repaired. You may not want to look too closely at the extent of the damage sin has had in your life. You may have convinced yourself that you don't have a sin problem, yet you know that something is wrong with the wall around your heart.

The good news is that freedom can be yours through Jesus Christ. He offers freedom from the damage of sin and will help you repair the crumbling walls of your heart. To experience this, though, you must be willing to listen to the truth that He brings.

The Truth About Biblical Truth

What is true? We've heard lots of claims made about the Bible and God. Which are reliable and which are false? Every day we are faced with choosing the truth or a lie, but how can we tell which is which?

First, the truth is dependable. False claims crumble over time, but the truth stands firm. Romans 3:4 says that truth is dependable and faithful. It doesn't matter who believes it or who rejects it—truth is truth. No matter what the people around you say, no matter what you hear on the news or on social media, the only messenger you can depend upon is God. If He says something is true, it cannot be anything but true.

What if some were unfaithful? Does their faithlessness nullify the faithfulness of God? By no means! Let God be true though every one were a liar, as it is written, "That you may be justified in your words, and prevail when you are judged."

—Romans 3:3–4

God's truth doesn't pivot on my opinion or my circumstances, and it doesn't change with trends or world events. The Bible says the Word of the Lord stands forever (Isaiah 40:8, 1 Peter 1:25), so we can count on it. God's Word and His promises are the only truths that will remain.

Second, truth is real. Hebrews 8:1–2 says that "we have such a high priest [Christ], one who is seated at the right hand of the throne of the Majesty in heaven, a minister in the holy places, in the true tent that the Lord set up, not man." Church buildings are wonderful, but they aren't *the* church. They aren't *the* tabernacle that God is building up in heaven. We are!

As believers, we are the body of Christ; we are His church. As His children, we know His voice. We know the truth of the great change manifested in our lives as a result of being given the gift of the Holy Spirit upon receiving Christ.

Third, the truth bears good fruit and lasting results. How we live our lives demonstrates whether we are truly in Him. If we live to please our flesh, doing what we want, then, according to Galatians 5:19–21, our lives will be full of strife, envy, rebellion, perversion, discontent, and the like. The Word goes on to say that if we live for Christ, by contrast, we will bear the joyful, life-giving, satisfying fruit of His Spirit (Galatians 5:22–24).

First John 3 lays out the straightforward reality: those

who continue in sin do not know Christ, and those who do know Him prove it by keeping God's commandments.

As the Gospel of John explains, God is the true vine and we are the branches (John 15:5). A branch cannot live on its own. A branch cannot support itself. It needs to be attached to a source of life (John 15:4). When a branch is unattached to the vine, it isn't good for anything—it is only to be thrown away and burned (John 15:6).

When we are unattached from the truth found in Christ, our lives will not produce true fruit and we will never find freedom or fulfillment. If we abide in Him, content to be branches plugged into the vine that gives life, we will naturally produce the fruit of the Spirit that shows our commitment to Christ (John 15:5).

Christ called Himself the true bread of life. If we know Him, we are living on the bread of life—bread that will give us true sustenance and lasting fulfillment (John 6:48). There is no fulfillment in people, in buildings, or in careers. However, there is fulfillment in Christ.

So many people are tired of the trivial and the fake, and they are desperately searching for something real. Jesus, along with the truth He offers, is right there in front of them, but we as believers need to pray that the Holy Spirit opens the eyes of those who are searching.

How Easily We Forget

Going back to the passage in John 8, it's interesting to note that the Jewish men who insisted they had never been enslaved had forgotten all about the terrible time of slavery that Israel had endured centuries before their conversation with Jesus took place. They didn't know their own history. They didn't know *truth*.

Look at what Jesus tells them in John 8:43: "Why do you not understand what I say? It is because you cannot bear to hear my word." Just as we can be blinded to the light of Christ, we can be deaf to His truth if we let the messages of the world drown Him out.

Jesus didn't mince words with these men. He told them clearly that they were listening to the Devil, the father of lies, and ignoring the voice of truth standing right in front of them (John 8:44–46). I'm sure He got their attention when He said, "Whoever is of God hears the words of God. The reason why you do not hear them is that you are not of God" (John 8:47).

If we are His followers—if we seek Christ as our source of life and put Him first—we won't have to search for the truth. We'll know the truth, and the truth will set us free (John 8:32).

The Truth Will Expose All

Gang members talk about owning a city or a block or a street. They act like it's theirs, but did they pay for that city block? Is their name on the deed?

This happens in the church, too. It's easy to think that we have ownership over a congregation or a building or a church. It's easy to think that we belong, but the Bible says that in the end, people will come and say, "Lord, Lord didn't we cast out demons, didn't we do this in your name?" And God will say that he never knew us!

> *Not everyone who says to me, "Lord, Lord," will enter the kingdom of heaven, but the one who does the will of my Father who is in heaven. On that day many will say to me, "Lord, Lord, did we not prophesy in your name, and cast out demons in your name, and do many mighty works in your name?" And then will I declare to them, "I never knew you; depart from me, you workers of lawlessness."*
>
> **—Matthew 7:21–23**

Jesus described what it's like to be exposed to the truth of the Word of God yet not live by it. Are you going to receive the truth of Christ? Are you going to hold on to it? Will you trust His truth enough to live by it?

Don't be like those questioners in John 8, whose ears were so closed to the truth that they missed the answer to life even when Jesus—who *was* and *is* the answer—was speaking directly to them. Hold fast to Christ and His Word, and the walls of your heart will prove strong because they have a foundation of truth.

Chapter Five Questions

Question: What is false freedom? Why do people sometimes think they are free when they aren't?

_____

_____

_____

_____

_____

_____

_____

_____

_____

_____

_____

_____

Question: What are ways people try to break free from the slavery of sin on their own? Have you ever tried to find deliverance apart from Christ and His truth? What was the result?

_____

_____

_____

_____

_____

_____

_____

_____

_____

_____

_____

Question: What are the three traits of biblical truth? How can they help you discern truth in a variety of situations?

_____

_____

_____

_____

_____

_____

_____

_____

_____

_____

_____

_____

Action: To what extent is your life ruled by truth? Recommit yourself to the Word through a daily Bible reading plan. If you are already in the Bible daily, build on that with a Scripture memory plan.

Chapter Five Notes

CHAPTER SIX

Forgotten Testimony

Now the angel of the LORD *went up from Gilgal to Bochim. And he said, "I brought you up from Egypt and brought you into the land that I swore to give to your fathers. I said, 'I will never break my covenant with you, and you shall make no covenant with the inhabitants of this land; you shall break down their altars.' But you have not obeyed my voice. What is this you have done? So now I say, I will not drive them out before you, but they shall become thorns in your sides, and their gods shall be a snare to you." As soon as the angel of the* LORD *spoke these words to all the people of Israel, the people lifted up their voices and wept.*
—Judges 2:1–4

One of the most important things we can do to continue growing in Christ is to stay mindful of all the Lord has done for us and walk daily in that truth. It is easy to get comfortable in our present condition. We become so used to being redeemed that we forget that we ever needed rescuing.

If we become complacent in our comfort, we can subconsciously distance ourselves from God and our dependency on Him. Objects or people start creeping into the place reserved for God alone. When our walls are crumbling around us and we stop seeing God as the One who can restore them, either we've grown so comfortable with the mess that we no longer notice it, or we have forgotten what our walls should look like.

In Judges 2, an angel of the Lord reminded the Israelites of everything God had done for them (Judges 2:1–3). God had delivered them from slavery in Egypt, provided for them in the desert, and led them into the promised land. Joshua had consistently modeled a life of worship to God as Israel's leader. But he was at the end of his life, and in Judges 2:6–8, it says that he dismissed all of the Israelites to their own inheritances and died soon after.

It didn't take long for the people of Israel to forget how wonderful God is. The Scriptures say they did what was evil in God's sight and worshiped false gods (Judges 2:11). They forgot all He had done and all that He had given them. You see, they remembered for a time, but when new generations arose, these generations weren't taught about God. They didn't know the truth.

In Judges, Joshua was a truth-teller for the people— and Moses and Abraham before him—but without someone pointing them to the one true God, the Israelites were quick to abandon their faith.

Be a Truth-Teller

We've been talking about the truth of Christ, reminding each other that the truth isn't found anywhere else but in Him. It's great if we understand and embrace that truth, but having faith ourselves isn't enough. One of our roles is to share the truth of Christ with others, to lead future generations, and to pass on to them all we have learned about God. We must do everything we can to ensure that the following generations don't forget about the Lord's goodness and provision like the Israelites did after Joshua was gone (Judges 2:12).

We are called to share the truth, to be bold with God's Word and quick to share stories about the miraculous works He has done. But sadly, we oftentimes do a terrible job.

It used to be that the storytellers, the ones who imparted wisdom and history to future generations, were the most revered members of society. Now, we view them as timewasters. We tease them for talking about the past and not the present. We may even cringe when they launch into one of their stories. The days of sitting on the front porch for hours while the older members of the family tell stories about years past are disappearing as we busily rush off to the next activity on the list.

We are a society who has become mindless. We don't want to remember or think or plan or sit with our thoughts and our memories. We want to be entertained. We want movies and TV and games and apps. We are told what to think, how to think, and what to think about. We are drowning in a sea of media messages, but few of them represent the truth

God isn't going to shout over all of that noise. He tells us, "Be still, and know that I am God" (Psalm 46:10). If you truly want to understand the truth well enough to be a truth teller to others, you will have to pick up God's Word.

You will have to sit before Him, both talking to Him and letting Him speak. God tells us to meditate on His Word day and night (Psalm 1:2), but too often our days and nights are filled with only falsehoods and worthless messages while the source of truth sits on our shelf collecting dust.

What Is Your Legacy?

The easiest and most obvious place to share truth and faith is within our own families. Do your children know about Jesus? Do they *know* Him?

> *And these words that I command you today shall be on your heart. You shall teach them diligently to your children, and shall talk of them when you sit in your house, and when you walk by the way, and when you lie down, and when you rise.*
>
> **—Deuteronomy 6:6–7**

Are you taking advantage of every opportunity to talk about the truth of God with your children, or are you wasting those opportunities? Are you leaving them a legacy of godliness or just a legacy of money and possessions? Are you training them to have the skills to build strong spiritual walls and where to go when they need repair?

Many young adults go to church with their parents when they are children, but as soon as they can choose for themselves, they stop going. They say they have a praying mama or a praying grandparent, or they remember there was always a Bible on the table of their home, but the truth of God isn't taught to them or modeled for them in the deliberate and compelling ways necessary to keep them practicing the faith into adulthood.

Judges 2:10 says that "there arose another generation after them who did not know the LORD or the work that he had done for Israel." You do understand that there is another generation coming, don't you? A large part of the work God has for us on this earth is spreading His truth to younger generations, to keep Him at the center and encourage young people to give their lives to Him so that they can eventually do that same for the next generation that comes along.

We need to do more than pray for the younger generations. We need to get them in the Word. We need to open their eyes to the truth of Jesus. We need to show them *why* He's our Savior and why we cry when we raise our hands to Him. We need to seek opportunities to share our stories of God's faithfulness—to sit on the front porch or around the dinner table and share the truth that has transformed us and can change their future as well.

Your Testimony Matters

All of this comes down to sharing our testimony with others. The first step is knowing your testimony, and the second step is becoming comfortable communicating it with others. Maybe you want to write it down, remembering who you were when you were lost in your sin and recounting what Jesus did to rescue you and bring you into the light (Ephesians 5:8). You may also want to practice by giving your testimony to someone in your family—a loved one who may not even know all of your story and will be encouraged by hearing it.

Peter wrote these instructions to believers: "…always be prepared to give an answer to everyone who asks you to give the reason for the hope that you have" (1 Peter 3:15 NIV). Are you prepared to give an answer? There are people all around you who desperately need the truth that you have. You can be the one to throw a life raft to a man or woman in desperate need of rescue.

As we grow in our faith, we recognize how Christ gave so much for us. We see the benefit of giving and not just receiving. One of the ways that we give is to share our testimony with younger generations—or with anyone we know who needs God's grace and forgiveness. We need to pray for opportunities to share with them all the riches we have learned, all the struggles He has helped us through, and all the truth He has revealed. They may not even know it, but they are hungry for truth, and the more they consume empty, counterfeit media messages, the hungrier they become.

This is how we give back. This is how we groom the next generation. And you know what? This is how we overcome: by the blood of the Lamb and the word of our testimony (Revelation 12:11)! God will use your testimony to raise up new leaders. All He is asking you to do is trust Him and be prepared to share His truth with those around you.

You can be a truth teller like Joshua. You can be part of changing the world for Christ by developing new movers and shakers who will invest in the next generation, and the next, and the next.

As you share your testimony, you'll probably find yourself being blessed by your own story. God has done so much for each of us, yet we sometimes forget the depths of His love and mercy. By telling your own story, you acknowledge God as the strengthener of your foundation and the one who repairs the crumbling walls of your life.

Yes, It Is Our Problem to Fix

Proverbs 30 shows us an example of a faithless generation. The chapter describes people who curse their fathers and their mothers, who are filthy even if they are clean in their own eyes, whose "teeth are swords, whose fangs are knives" (Proverbs 30:14). They don't acknowledge God with their words or their actions, because they have lost sight of who the Lord is and what He has done for them. It is our job as believers to do everything we can to prevent such an outcome.

In particular, we must invest in today's generations. We must teach the truth and raise up truth-tellers.

These are the commands, decrees and laws the LORD your God directed me to teach you to observe in the land that you are crossing the Jordan to possess, so that you, your children and their children after them may fear the LORD your God as long as you live by keeping all his decrees and commands that I give you, and so that you may enjoy long life.

—Deuteronomy 6:1–2 *(NIV)*

Too many believers of all ages are complacent, concerned only for what they can get from the Lord rather than what they can give Him. God is calling us to adjust our thinking. He calls on us to realize that, just as Jesus came to serve and not to be served, we have been put on earth to give—not just our resources and our time, but our stories.

We need to be models of giving ourselves away for the Lord. When the younger generation learns that Jesus really is a Servant-King, and that He watches us live for Him and share our testimonies of His faithfulness, the result will be transformative.

Our children need to hear us giving Him praise for everything in our lives. They need to hear us say that God is good all the time, whether we're working or playing, whether times are hard or abundant. They need to hear us singing praise to the Lord, thanking Him every day for His blessings. We can show them what it looks like to have hearts of gratitude and trust so that when they are living on their own, they will build their own lives on the foundation of Christ. While you still have the chance, show them how to put Christ first, and always pray faithfully that God will captivate their hearts.

God has given us an assignment: to remind every generation of His faithfulness and help turn their hearts toward Him. What a privilege to be used by Him! Pray about the ways you could share God's love and truth with the people in your family or your sphere of influence. Prepare your testimony. Seek opportunities. Be part of helping to change the world for Christ.

Chapter Six Questions

Question: What strengths do you observe, and what concerns arise, as you consider the way your family and your church family seem to understand and practice their faith?

_____

_____

_____

_____

_____

_____

_____

_____

_____

_____

_____

Question: What stories from the past (from relatives, older church members, or Christian biographies) have impacted your life for Christ?

_____

_____

_____

_____

_____

_____

_____

_____

_____

_____

_____

Question: In what ways are you passing on the truth to the next generation? What are some additional ways to train younger believers that you can begin implementing in your life and ministry?

_____

_____

_____

_____

_____

_____

_____

_____

_____

_____

_____

Action: Write out your testimony, including how you came to faith in Christ and important points of how you have grown, experienced God's faithfulness, etc. Share a copy with other members of your family or church.

Chapter Six Notes

CHAPTER SEVEN

It's Now or Never

For the time has come for judgment to begin at the house of God; and if it begins with us first, what will be the end of those who do not obey the gospel of God? Now "If the right-eous one is scarcely saved, where will the ungodly and the sinner appear?"

—1 Peter 4:17–18 *(NKJV)*

It's every guy's fear: he gets down on one knee and opens a blue box to reveal a sparkly diamond. "Will you marry me?" he asks the girl of his dreams.

She hesitates, her face unsure. Then she says those dreaded words, "I'm going to have to think about it."

Jesus's invitation to commit to Him is far weightier than a marriage proposal, yet we often walk through life with an uncommitted attitude: "I'm going to have to think about it." But the time is now, and He is inviting you into abundant life.

In this book, we have uncovered truth, and we have looked at our roles in communicating that truth to others.

But all of this comes up short if we aren't living our lives in the best way possible—surrendered to Christ and resistant to the worldly influences that keep us from His will. Peter's words make it clear that we need to get serious about living right before God.

You may be a better housekeeper than I am. I have no great love of vacuuming, washing the dishes, or doing yard work. I'd rather put it off than stay on top of it. It's only when the dust has accumulated or the weeds have grown tall that I get motivated to take care of my housekeeping business.

This is often the same attitude we have about maintaining our spiritual walls. We don't care too much about caring for them until disaster strikes and we look around at the crumbling mess. Just like with house maintenance, we must continue working daily at our walk with God to keep it in good order.

The Big Five

The questions Peter asks in the above passage are sobering. Scripture has plenty to say about avoiding the traps that will pull us away from Christ and toward the world. In 1 Corinthians 10:6–10, the Bible gives us five historical examples of the sins that undermine our influence and our effectiveness as believers.

> *Now these things became our examples, to the intent that we should not lust after evil things as they also lusted. And do not become idolaters as were some of them. As it is written, "The people sat down to eat and drink, and rose up to play." Nor let us commit sexual immorality, as some of*

*them did, and in one day twenty-three thousand fell; nor
let us tempt Christ, as some of them also tempted, and were
destroyed by serpents; nor complain, as some of them also
complained, and were destroyed by the destroyer.*
—1 Corinthians 10:6–10 *(NKJV)*

The first pitfall we must avoid is *lusting after evil
things* (1 Corinthians 10:6 NKJV). Paul asked his readers
to recall the Israelites wandering the desert in the Old Tes-
tament, who forsook their faith in God and instead
adopted the sinful practices of the world around them.
They lusted after evil, and it led them away from God.
Paul explained, "These things took place as examples for
us, that we might not desire evil as they did" (1 Corinthians 10:6). If we keep our eyes on Christ, our desire for
evil things will diminish.

There are so many things in life that our hearts long to
chase. Some of them we know are bad right from the start,
but it doesn't stop us from wanting them. It's tempting to
let our minds sneak over to these things and fantasize
about them while keeping our hands clean. We look
around and think we're fine since we didn't technically
sin. Yet, thinking about sinful things longingly is just as
much a sin as going out and doing them.

The next warning Paul outlines in this passage is to
avoid *idolatry,* which at its core is selfishness. If we make
any worldly thing an idol, we are doing so because we
want to put ourselves on the throne and worship whatever
we think is worthy. The passage says that "the people sat
down to eat and drink and rose up to play" (1 Corinthians
10:7). They were receiving blessings from God's hands,
but after they partook of the meal, they got up and ran

back after their idols. They forgot about the faithfulness of God along their journey.

Anytime we put something ahead of God, we are turning it into an idol. We even do this with really good things. We idolize our children, our work, our leisure, and how we serve others. We tend to make idols out of comfort, power, approval, and control. All sorts of sinful behaviors grow from these roots. It takes constant vigilance to stay free from idols.

The next area that can lead Christians astray, and one that damages churches and families in America on a daily basis, is *sexual immorality*. Paul's warning is backed up with evidence of how God feels about people who use sex only for their own pleasure. He wrote, "We must not indulge in sexual immorality as some of them did, and twenty-three thousand fell in a single day" (1 Corinthians 10:8). God is serious about His people honoring Him with their bodies.

God made marriage to represent His relationship with His people. It is the lifelong commitment between us and Him. Anytime sex is not between a husband and a wife, the Bible tells us it is sinful. This includes both sex outside of marriage and sex in marriage that doesn't involve (only) a husband and a wife.

The fourth sinful practice that can harm our relationship with God and destroy our witness is *tempting God*, or putting God to the test (1 Corinthians 10:9). I would also call this "disrespecting Christ," and it includes taking His name in vain, joking about Him, or trying to see how much you can get away with. If you are trying to determine where God's line in the sand is so that you can dance right up to the edge of it, you are guilty of tempting God.

Finally, Paul warns us about *grumbling and complaining* (1 Corinthians 10:10). This doesn't seem like such a big deal at first, but remember that the Israelites in the wilderness were grumblers. They became a cancer, dragging down everyone around them and putting up a barrier between God and his people (Numbers 14:29).

Complaining and negative talk have a way of spreading and infecting a community, and there is no place for these habits among God's people. It grieves God's heart when He gives us good things and we can only complain about them. It keeps us from seeing the truth about God's blessings in our lives.

Keeping Focus

These are harsh truths. But God needs to have witnesses here on earth who strive to do what is right, what is just, and what is pure. We need to pray that God will open our eyes to what is going on around us, because this world is so accustomed to sin and disobedience that even believers don't see the problem much of the time. People justify what they do, deny their sinful behavior, or try to twist things around so that wrong looks like right. But as followers of Christ, we cannot afford to be fooled.

We're here to show the way. The faith mindset means having trust and confidence in God. It means turning from evil, even when we're so very tempted by it. How can we be the light of the world if we let ourselves be taken over by the darkness (Matthew 5:14)?

We are called to speak truth and model faith in God,

even when it seems like we are alone in our desire to live for Christ. God promises to be with His people and give them strength as they stand up for Him in a fallen world. We are all called to pull off that bushel basket that is covering our lives and shine for Him (Matthew 5:15–16). The world is watching us.

Keeping our focus on Christ means not causing others to fall into sin. We aren't living in obedience if we worry only about ourselves and ignore our brothers and sisters who are being dragged down by the world's temptations. Later in 1 Corinthians, Paul describes the sin that lies ready to tempt each one of us:

> *Therefore let him who thinks he stands take heed lest he fall. No temptation has overtaken you except such as is common to man; but God is faithful, who will not allow you to be tempted beyond what you are able, but with the temptation will also make the way of escape, that you may be able to bear it.*
> **—1 Corinthians 10:12–13** *(NKJV)*

Hold on to this promise. God knows that we live in a difficult time, with temptations threatening to ensnare us at every turn. But if we look to Him as our guide, He will provide an escape route every time. We need to put our faith in God's ability to deliver us from temptation.

We also need to pray for those around us and remind them that the world's snares do not have to trap them. God can rescue anyone, even those who feel like they are too far down the road of sinful behavior. Because of Jesus, we have a way out, and our sin doesn't have to define us.

A Matter of the Heart

God knows the heart. He knows your motives, and He knows where your mind is. As Paul said, "I want to do what is good, but I don't. I don't want to do what is wrong, but I do it anyway" (Romans 7:19 NLT). We can all relate to this tug-of-war in our soul, and this struggle is why we need God. It is why we must be vigilant and committed to knowing God's Word and staying in fellowship with God's people through the church.

In 1 Peter 4:19, Scripture says, "Therefore let those who suffer according to the will of God commit their souls to Him in doing good, as to a faithful Creator" (NKJV). You might have been through some persecution for the sake of Christ, and you may be suffering a trial for Him right now. But God's calling is on our lives to serve Him wholeheartedly, and when we do that, we will understand true peace and joy in Him.

Anyone who flies an airplane know that when a plane is taking off down a runway, it reaches a point after which there is no turning back. The force of the plane and the power of the engines are so great that the plane has to lift off no matter what. In aeronautics jargon, that "point of no return" is called V1.[2]

When you come into the body of Christ, it's V1 time! Your mission is clear, and God has promised to strengthen you in your obedience. Proclaim that it's V1 time for your faith: time to push forward, full throttle, no stopping, no turning back!

Trials will most definitely come if we are truly living for the Lord in this world, which wants to deny truth. But the good news is this: God has given us a blueprint of how to live in an abundance of righteousness, peace, and joy. It's going to be tough. We're going to fall short. But we must commit ourselves to doing good, nevertheless.

We must be the example that He expects us to be so that the world can see what it means to live in truth. We want to feel the urgency to fulfill God's plan for our lives—to say to the Lord, "I don't want to leave this world until I know I have given my whole heart to living into Your destiny for me."

We can't be casual about obeying Him! The stakes are too high.

Our Lives Should Match Our Beliefs

Imagine dropping off your laundry at a one-hour dry cleaner. The one-hour guarantee is clearly displayed on the sign. You tell the clerk, "See you in one hour."

And she tells you to come back in two days. You were already on your way out the door, but you turn around, confused. What happened to one hour?

"Oh," she says, "That's just the name of the business. We aren't really a one-hour dry cleaner. We just liked the way it looked on our sign."

Christians are sometimes like this. We call ourselves Christians. We go to church, and we say all the right things, but when it comes down to it, we're not committed to Christ. We aren't committed to living the life God expects of us. We have one foot in the Kingdom of God and one foot in the world, and we are too scared or too entangled by our sin to go Vl—to make a decision to live for

Christ full throttle, no matter what.

If you are feeling like your spiritual walls have gradually crumbled all around you, this may be an indication that you're stuck in the pitfall of noncommitment. Perhaps you were once excited about living for Christ, but over time your passion has waned and your light has all but gone out.

You may go to church every Sunday and carry your Bible around for all to see. You may wear a Christian t-shirt, put a Christian sticker on your car, or post Bible verses on social media. But the way you live out your life conveys something completely different.

When questioned about it, like the dry cleaner, you may even try to justify the difference between your outward display and your inward life. "Nobody really acts like that," you might say. "The Bible was written two thousand years ago, and no one can really follow it in today's world."

If you have the Holy Spirit within you, you know the truth (1 John 2:27). You know that God's truth is the only truth and that living for Him wholeheartedly is His plan for your life. You know that if you trust Him, He will show you how to resist temptation and give your life away for Him. You know that true peace, joy, and purpose are only found in the center of God's will. This is your chance to commit fully. Now is the time to go all the way.

Chapter Seven Questions

Question: What were the five big sins that Israel committed? Which is the greatest temptation for you?

_____

_____

_____

_____

_____

_____

_____

_____

_____

_____

_____

Question: How does God help us overcome temptation? How does being "V1" for Christ help us in the fight against sin?

_____

_____

_____

_____

_____

_____

_____

_____

_____

_____

Question: Why is it wise to learn many different skills? What skills do you have now? What skills do you need to add to your skill set?

_____

_____

_____

_____

_____

_____

_____

_____

_____

_____

_____

Action. Talk to older believers who have walked faithfully with the Lord for many years. Ask them to share ways that God has enabled them to overcome temptation in their life.

Chapter Seven Notes

_____

_____

_____

_____

_____

_____

_____

_____

_____

_____

_____

_____

_____

_____

_____

_____

_____

_____

_____

_____

_____

_____

CHAPTER EIGHT

Rise to the Challenge

Therefore lift your drooping hands and strengthen your weak knees, and make straight paths for your feet, so that what is lame may not be put out of joint but rather be healed.
—Hebrews 12:12–13

When we are wounded, it is tempting to retreat in isolation and shut out the rest of the world. Introspection in isolation oftentimes robs us of our joy. However, it is a great paradox that when, instead of retreating, we reach out to serve others, we find ourselves restored.

Let's turn back to Nehemiah, the committed man of God who risked persecution and took great risks to rebuild the walls in Jerusalem (Nehemiah 2:5). We have been spending time rebuilding our walls, replacing our old selves with the truth of Jesus Christ, replacing our old habits with godly ones, and turning our passive faith into active faith.

But it isn't enough simply to rebuild our walls. There

is one key element we need to work into the design of those walls: we need to build a gate (Nehemiah 3).

Your Heart's Gate

There are people within the body of Christ who have no gates. They have walled themselves in, protecting themselves from the world, but there is no way for them to pour into others' lives, nor is there a way for them to let others in.

Then there are believers whose gates keep getting destroyed by the enemy. The Devil goes in and out as he chooses. Worldly values and perspectives easily infiltrate their hearts, giving place to compromise and confusion. Neither type of person knows how to rise to the challenge or how to say, "Enough is enough!"

Sometimes when we have been wounded by others, we seal up our gates to protect our hearts. But that isn't God's plan for us. He wants us to let others in so that they can experience the radical love of Jesus, and He wants us to have the freedom that comes from opening our hearts.

Sometimes attacks from the enemy seem to be so relentless that we just stop fighting. Other times, the attacks are so subtle that, before we know it, our gate has been destroyed. The enemy knows how to prey on our vulnerabilities and hit our weak spots.

Yet God has equipped us to withstand these attacks and to experience victory over an enemy He has already defeated! It's not too late—all is not lost. Your gate can be rebuilt and your defenses restored.

A gate is a place that allows for entry and exit. It serves

a vital function and requires particular care. So, my friends, it's time to work on our gates.

It's one thing to decide you need to work on your gate; it's another thing to start building. It's one thing to say, "Lord, I love You," but it's another thing to go out and love others in risky ways for the sake of Christ. It's one thing to say, "I'm sorry," but it's another thing to do good to those who have persecuted or abused you.

There is something about putting actions behind our words that allows us to rise to the challenge. Have you heard about a ministry opportunity that makes your heart beat a little bit faster, but you are afraid to step into it? Do you have a friend or a neighbor who is lost without Christ, but you are hesitant to get involved? God is calling us to love Him through our actions, and sometimes we have to take that first step out of obedience before we experience His blessing.

Nehemiah knew this. He knew that if he could get the people *moving,* then things would be different for Jerusalem. Everyone worked together to rebuild the gates (Nehemiah 4:6). Everyone took an active role, and they did it together. They were opposed by others in Jerusalem, and I'm sure there were many days they were afraid, or tired, and wanted to stay in bed. But God called them to holy action, and they obeyed.

God is calling you to holy action! Are you ready to obey? It is by obedience that gates are rebuilt. It is through daily fellowship with God and regular fellowship with other believers that obedience is encouraged and gates are strengthened. As we live life God's way, surrendering all areas of our lives to Him, we find ourselves guarding our hearts with all diligence and joining with other believers to press on in faith.

Keeping On

Nehemiah and the people helping him with the building project were subjected to all kinds of verbal abuse—and worse (Nehemiah 4:1–3). Several foreign armies started to plot against Nehemiah to stop his efforts (Nehemiah 4:7–8).

His response to this persecution was the same response we should have: he prayed and asked God to be His protection. In Nehemiah 4:14, he reassured the people with these words: "Do not be afraid of them. Remember the LORD, who is great and awesome, and fight for your brothers, your sons, your daughters, your wives, and your homes."

Do you see opposition rising up around you—in your church, in your workplace, in your community, or even in your family? Is your first inclination to be afraid? These words from Nehemiah are for you. He knew that God was mightier than any armies that opposed him, and he knew he could not fail if he was carrying out God's clear plan for his life.

We know the world has attacked the church. We know we have targets on our backs. But we must keep on! We must do the good work that God has called us to do.

We must keep rising. We must press in and fight for truth, for marriages, for families, and for godliness.

After all of that opposition, as the people were working on the wall and looking over their shoulder, waiting for armies to attack, something amazing happened. In Nehe-miah 4:15, we read: "And it happened, when our enemies heard that it was known to us, and that God had brought their plot to nothing, that all of us returned to the wall, everyone to his work" (NKJV).

God will work out the details, my friends. It's our job to rise to the challenge.

Double Duty

Nehemiah divided his labor force in half to ensure that the job kept progressing while the Israelites stayed safe (Nehemiah 4:16). He assigned half of his crew to work on the construction and half to stand guard with spears, shields, bows, and armor (Nehemiah 4:16).

Sometimes rising to the challenge means doing two things at once. It means building your family while you're on your knees. It means being a faithful worker during the week and then having energy on Sunday to worship God at church.

Nehemiah trusted God completely, and he was wise in his leadership. He instructed the workers to carry heavy loads with one arm and wield their weapon with the other (Nehemiah 4:17). He made sure that the man who sounded the trumpet was right beside him, and he set up a guard near the wall day and night (Nehemiah 4:18). But he never lost sight of the One who was really fighting for the wall. As he told the people in Nehemiah 4:20, "In the place where you hear the sound of the trumpet, rally to us there. Our God will fight for us."

The people helping Nehemiah were armed and ready

day and night, and they stayed vigilant because they knew what they were fighting for. In the same way, God is always preparing you to do battle for His sake.

Do you know what you're fighting for? You may face a battleground in your family, in your job, or within your own heart (if you are fighting temptation). When you come to church, you should be arming yourself for battle as you learn to be a better man or woman, perhaps a better husband or wife, and a more faithful follower of Jesus.

Church isn't just the place where we come to hear good music, listen to preaching, and see our friends. It is our battle camp, where we come to be reminded that God will fight for us while we focus on arming ourselves for the battles that await us in the coming week. Don't become lazy and think that you are not part of a battle! The Devil is a prowling lion who will pounce if he sees you put down your weapon (1 Peter 5:8).

Keeping Watch

It's time for us to rise to the challenge—to arm ourselves to take on the forces of this world that threaten to drag down our children or pressure the church to squeeze itself into the world's mold.

Here is our mission: We are going to serve as Christ served. We are going to do as Christ did. We are going to spread the Word of God and shine His light so that men may see His love and truth in our good works and glorify our Father in heaven. Remember Nehemiah's reassurance—"Our God will fight for us" (Nehemiah 4:20).

Nehemiah 7 reminds us that rising to the challenge

means to be vigilant. The wall was finished, but Nehemiah appointed faithful men to guard the gates and instructed the people to keep the gates closed until the heat of the day (Nehemiah 7:3). He was called to build the walls because the city of Jerusalem was important to God, and he didn't let his guard down once that construction project was complete. He knew that the city needed gates to function, but he also knew the gates could make it vulnerable, so he instructed the people to keep watch.

Keeping watch in your own life means protecting your inner city: your heart. So, keep watch over what you let into your heart and your mind. It also means protecting your family, protecting the new believers in your midst, and speaking God's truth to those around you. By staying faithful in prayer and studying God's Word, you will be setting out watchmen to look over the weak and to make sure that the gates stay strong.

If you can guard your heart and keep the walls safe through prayer and the Word, you will be equipped to build others up. If you are vigilant about your own walls and gates, you will find you have a stable foundation from which you can share the good news with a hurting world.

We must stay vigilant. Remember that the enemy is crafty, and he is always looking for a weakness in our gates that he can exploit.

Taking It In

Rising to the challenge also means being hungry for the Word. Imagine if people were lined up outside your church building every Sunday, waiting for the doors to open, yearning for the time when they would be hearing the Word of God? That's what was going on with Nehemiah. The people craved Scripture!

In Nehemiah 8:1, Ezra the scribe brought the book of the law of Moses to the Water Gate, and the people crowded in to hear it (Nehemiah 8:3). This was a big event! Think about the enthusiasm inside a football stadium on game day—but instead of waiting for kickoff, the people gathered are waiting, excited, to hear the truths from God's Word.

Do we realize how blessed we are to have a stack of Bibles in our house? We have constant access to God's truth right in our hands, but so often, we take it for granted.

In Psalm 42:1, the psalmist says, "As the deer pants for streams of water, so my soul pants for you, my God" (NIV). Do we crave the Word of God in that way? Does God's truth fill us with joy and prompt us to worship? Nehemiah 8:6 tells us that as Ezra opened the book, the people "bowed their heads and worshiped the LORD with their faces to the ground." The Word of God should inspire reverence, and the truth it contains should strengthen us as we strive to rise to God's challenge for our lives.

Great Defenders

There is a need in the body of Christ for those who are ready to work and defend the faith. We need people who care about nothing more than serving Christ. The workers who helped Nehemiah were completely focused on rebuilding the wall so that God would be glorified. Their hearts were not divided. For most of us, serving Christ is just another calendar square in our day, not a calling that captures our whole heart.

We need Christians who are fed up with the status quo. We need people who are frustrated with the state of the world—people who know there is a better way to live. We need to put aside the petty differences that divide us as believers and band together to do God's work. I'm sure that some of Nehemiah's volunteers disagreed with each other about small things, but they didn't let small disputes get in the way of the big picture.

Remember that Nehemiah wrote about how every one of the builders had his sword guarded at his side as he rebuilt the walls (Nehemiah 4:18). These men were ready to fight even as they were carefully rebuilding their city. We must make sure the walls of God's church are stable and secure. We must guard the gates and continue to battle for truth. We have a mission that requires our undivided attention, and God is ready to fight for us when we step into that calling boldly.

We must build strong gates and then defend them daily. And as our walls grow stronger, we must reach out to help those around us defend and strengthen their own gates—so that the body of Christ, collectively, shines brighter.

Chapter Eight Questions

Question: What is the significance of spiritual "gates"? How do they provide a balance between spiritual isolation and being ransacked by the enemy?

_____

_____

_____

_____

_____

_____

_____

_____

_____

_____

_____

Question: Where do you experience opposition to following God and His plan for you? How can you remain motivated to keep rising to the challenge?

_____

_____

_____

_____

_____

_____

_____

_____

_____

_____

_____

Question: What does it mean to "keep watch" over your life? How do you accomplish this?

_____

_____

_____

_____

_____

_____

_____

_____

_____

_____

_____

Action: Do you crave Scripture as the Jews of Nehemiah's day did? For one week, replace your regular car or home listening (music, podcasts, etc.) with an audio recording of Scripture. Take note of any differences in your attitude or of any insights that you learn through this exercise.

Chapter Eight Notes

_____

_____

_____

_____

_____

_____

_____

_____

_____

_____

_____

_____

_____

_____

_____

_____

_____

_____

_____

_____

_____

_____

_____

_____

CHAPTER NINE

Molded by God

This is the word that came to Jeremiah from the LORD: "Go down to the potter's house, and there I will give you my message." So I went down to the potter's house, and I saw him working at the wheel. But the pot he was shaping from the clay was marred in his hands; so the potter formed it into another pot, shaping it as seemed best to him. Then the word of the LORD came to me. He said, "Can I not do with you, Israel, as this potter does?" declares the LORD. "Like clay in the hand of the potter, so are you in my hand, Israel."

—Jeremiah 18:1–6 (NIV)

Imagine a potter working away to make a pot. He has a plan and a purpose for this particular blob of wet, dull clay in his hand. As he moves it and molds it, he is in complete control over what happens to the clay.

Now, imagine if the clay started talking back. What if it complained about being turned into a cup, insisting it become a vase instead? What if the clay refused to be painted blue? What if the clay grew angry with the potter and hardened so that it was totally useless?

It's a pretty ridiculous idea, yet this is often the way our hearts are towards our divine Potter. We must respond to the pressure of His hands and accept the hue He chooses for us if we want to be useful. Our crumbling walls will never be restored if we demand that the Potter make us into what we want rather than what He has designed for us to be.

There is a story of a little boy who toured Europe with his parents. They saw many cathedrals that had stained glass windows depicting various saints. When the family returned home, the parents asked the boy what he thought of the cathedrals. The boy answered, "I learned that saints are people the light shines through."[3]

Our lives may not be working out exactly as we hoped they would, but if we are living with complete faith in Christ, we can be confident that His light is shining through us. He uses us, as imperfect as we are, to shine His light in the darkness. We can trust that He is doing a good work in us and through us if we are committed to following Him (2 Corinthians 4:7 NIV).

As we study Jeremiah 18, we find three key habits that are vital for those who want to be molded and used by God: we are called to listen, obey, and serve.

Listen

The first discipline we need to develop as true disciples is that of listening. Jeremiah was called to be a prophet because his ears were attuned to God's voice, and the longer he served as God's messenger, the better he became at hearing the Lord speak. God called him to go down to the potter's house to hear His words (Jeremiah 18:1). It might have seemed like a strange errand for Jeremiah, but he knew God was instructing him to do it, so he didn't question it.

We must develop the habit of active listening. God is always speaking to us, but sometimes life can be so chaotic that we simply don't hear Him. Someone who is moldable knows that God is always working, every day, to bring shape, form, and beauty to life. Knowledge of the fact that God is always working, always moving, is enough for the moldable believer to stay alert and in tune with what God is telling him each and every day.

God is always speaking, but are we picking up on what He is saying? Are we trading a noisy, counterfeit life for a life of true communion with God?

Too often we come to God in prayer but do all the talking ourselves. Are you giving Him the time and space to speak to you? Do you give yourself times of quiet during the day when He can restore your soul and remind you of His truth?

Our worlds are often noisy, and we quickly lose the art of true listening. You may have to practice being still before God and listening to His voice, but like Jeremiah, you will find that your ears become more sensitive to Him the longer you walk with Him.

Obey

The second key habit we learn from Jeremiah is obedience. He promptly obeyed God's instructions to go to the potter's house, and when he went to watch the potter, he learned something that could repair the broken state of his people. He saw the potter working with a piece of clay on his wheel, but the clay spoiled in the potter's hand (Jeremiah 18:4). The potter put the clay back on the wheel and reworked it into another vessel, which symbolized God's willingness to restore us even when we have been broken by sin and rebellion (Jeremiah 18:4).

In Jeremiah 18:8, God said: "…and if that nation, concerning which I have spoken, turns from its evil, I will relent of the disaster that I intended to do to it." This indicates to us that what we choose right now, in this moment, is more important than all of the choices we have made leading up to this present one. In other words, we may have a lifetime of sin and disobedience behind us, but choosing obedience right now is enough to wipe our slates clean. What a beautiful picture of God's amazing grace!

Today we are free to experience all of God's blessings, no matter what you have done in the past. You might have shaken your fist at God hundreds of times, but all of that is in the past if you decide to obey Him right now.

Will you obey Him today? If God is pressing you, trying to move in your life to remold you the way a potter works his clay, will you be willing to be changed today? That's the question.

Nothing is preventing God from doing His great work in your life right here, right now, if you are willing to obey Him—today.

Serve

The third key discipline to develop is the habit of serving others. Jeremiah went to the potter's house alone, and he could have received the message he learned about God's willingness to rework the clay and kept it to himself. However, Jeremiah stayed true to his calling as a prophet to speak truth to people who were lost (Jeremiah 18:11).

Often, the people didn't want to hear what Jeremiah had to say, so they verbally abused Him. But he knew he was called to a life of service, even when he didn't get any glory for it.

Self-preservation is so appealing, isn't it? It's always a temptation to focus on what we want and what we need instead of asking God how He wants to use us each day. As we take each step, He gives us more opportunities. Jeremiah was obedient in going to the potter's house, and that obedience led him to an even greater assignment—to tell the people that God still wanted to redeem them and restore their relationship with Him.

Jeremiah wasn't always quick to serve. In Jeremiah 15:10, he complained to the Lord about the way the people mistreated him: "Woe is me, my mother, that you bore me, a man of strife and contention to the whole land!" But he was honest with God, and he listened to the truth when God spoke it to him. In the end, he was committed to God's call on his life even when things were hard.

We may *want* to sacrifice for others, but it's easy to talk ourselves out of it. We think we can only give our money once our own finances are in order. Or we are under the impression that we can only be a role model for other believers once we have our own relationship with God nailed down.

You may think your schedule is too busy or the time isn't exactly right for you to serve others, but the truth is, busyness can easily become a smoke screen when you're afraid to step out of your comfort zone.

In the middle of a chaotic life, it's crucial that you remain available to help others. Whatever God wants from you, can you make a commitment to Him that you will do it? Whomever you encounter that needs help, can you step in and meet the person's need? Can you vow that your purpose on this earth is to serve others for the sake of Christ?

We may not receive rewards or a pat on the back. Like Jeremiah, we may even be criticized or attacked for our service (Jeremiah 18:18). But true service is giving selflessly to others without expectation of any personal benefit.

The moldable believer understands that serving others first is what will bring him or her closer to God. We are never closer to Christ than when we are giving ourselves away the way He gave Himself for us. There is abundant life in serving others—in our willingness to be clay in the Potter's hand. Those who live a life of service know what Jeremiah knew: serving in obedience to God is the only truly fulfilling way to live.

Life in Truth

These three habits go hand in hand. By listening to God, you will know what He wants from you. Then, you can choose immediate obedience, and you can embrace the calling He has given you and use it to serve others.

Listening, obeying, and serving are three vital habits. If you rely on the Holy Spirit to give you strength and open doors for you, these habits can become a way of life. They will quickly put you on the path of living in truth and in true communion with Jesus Christ.

Chapter Nine Questions

Question: *Are we trading a noisy, counterfeit life for a life of true communion with God?* What does it take to truly listen to God? When do you hear Him most clearly? What noise in your life tends to drown out His still, small voice?

_____

_____

_____

_____

_____

_____

_____

_____

_____

Question: Are you actively obeying God today, or are you allowing past sins to keep you in defeat? In what area of obedience can you take action right now?

_____

_____

_____

_____

_____

_____

_____

_____

_____

_____

_____

Question: Are you serving now, or are you waiting until you have everything figured out? Has there been a time when someone blessed you who didn't "have it all together?" What is holding you back from helping others— and what is God's perspective on that hindrance?

_____

_____

_____

_____

_____

_____

_____

_____

_____

_____

_____

_____

Action: Write "Listen. Obey. Serve." on a piece of paper and put it where you will see it each morning. Make a habit of starting your day by listening to the Lord through His Word and prayer. As He reveals action steps and others' needs to you, obey Him and serve those He brings across your path.

Chapter Nine Notes

_____

_____

_____

_____

_____

_____

_____

_____

_____

_____

_____

_____

_____

_____

_____

_____

_____

_____

_____

_____

_____

_____

_____

CONCLUSION

Live in Freedom

But you are a chosen race, a royal priesthood, a holy na-
tion, a people for his own possession, that you may
proclaim the excellencies of him who called you out of
darkness into His marvelous light.
—1 Peter 2:9

We've been on an incredible journey. It can be difficult
to acknowledge that our lives are in disrepair. Yet our
grief can be the motivation that propels us into our greatest transformation.

We learned from Nehemiah that rebuilding our walls,
even in the wake of great devastation, is possible. When
the enemy tries to derail you, God will fight on your behalf. He wants to see you fortified, with all the idols
removed from your life. He longs to live in an open, loving relationship with you.

God wants us to live as far away from sin as possible
and to run back to Him when we mess up. He wants us to

live in freedom and has made that possible for us who believe in Him and follow His ways.

However, just as Israel so often forgot their years of slavery, we may tend to forget that God has delivered us from darkness into His marvelous light. When that happens, we find ourselves drifting from our connection to God. Before long, we have erected idols and strayed from our calling. Our spiritual walls crumble, and we are at a loss as to how to fix them on our own.

We must continually refocus on what it takes to stay in communion with God in order to maintain the walls of our hearts.

Seeking to know the truth revealed in God's Word and aligning our lifestyles with what God has for us are the foundation that everything else is built upon. Living by faith in this manner is the foundation for strong walls. It is a daily commitment of serving, obeying, and listening to the leading of the Holy Spirit.

Living a fortified life looks like raising the future generations to know and follow God and daring to go out into the world to be a light. When you have a solid foundation, you can extend your life to others. This is the ultimate example that Jesus set for us, for He came not to be served, but to serve and give His life a ransom to many (Matthew 20:28).

Are you ready to rebuild the walls of your life? Then begin today to follow in His steps.

REFERENCES

Notes

1. "A Story Is Told About Satan Having a Yard Sale." Contributed by Justin Meek. *Sermon Central.* June 6, 2001. https://www.sermoncentral.com/illustrations/sermon-illustration-justin-meek-stories-3040.

2. Hilkevitch, Jon. "Aircraft Speed into Danger Zone As They Pass Key Points on Takeoff." *Chicago Tribune.* July 27, 2000. http://articles.chicagotribune.com/2000-07-27/news/0007270400_1_takeoff-engine-fire-plane.

3. Albright, Joe. "Let the Light Shine Through." *Dial Hope.* October 6, 2017. http://www.dialhope.org/let-light-shine.

About the Author

Dr. Craig D. Hayes is a pastor who is chasing after God's heart and is humbled to serve as the founding pastor of CrossingPoint Christian Church in Missouri City and Rosharon, Texas. He is the delighted father of six children with Shannon, his lovely high school sweetheart and wife of twenty-five years.

Dr. Hayes is a lifelong learner who holds a master's degree in Christian administration from Atlantic Seminary, as well as a Doctorate of Divinity, and he is currently pursuing a Doctorate of Theology. He is also a Colson Fellow and serves as the Southwest District Overseer of Shepherd's Watch International Fellowship, based in

Houston, Texas.

It is Dr. Hayes's delight to serve the body of Christ as he works to stay true to his mission to make Jesus Christ not just a choice, but a lifestyle!

Made in the USA
Columbia, SC
29 March 2019